WITHIN THE SILENCE: FREEDOM GAINED
A PICTURED JOURNEY

BY DAVID MINTON

Published by: David Minton
PO. Box 147, Pike, NY, 14130
Publish rev.(4) date: 01/26/2021

Cover, Digitally Created Image: Within The Silence, by David Minton
Edited by Joyce Snyder

Minton, David
Within The Silence: Freedom Gained by David Minton
ISBN 978-1-77360546-3-5 (HC)
ISBN 978-1-77360546-4-2 (EPUB)

1. Minton, David 2. Religion, Spirituality

Other Books By Author

WITHIN THE SILENCE: LESSONS AND TRUST
ISBN 978-1-7360546-1-1 (SC)
ISBN 978-1-7360546-0-4 (HC)
ISBN 978-1-7360546-2-8 (EPUB)

Contents

Forward

This book of images is a continuation of a journey begun, containing previously released poems and some of the stories that led to the poems which came about because of spiritual experiences in my life. With some of the experiences, they were often difficult to articulate, so I began using images as a bridge to help express some aspect of a poem or story. In today's age, the Internet calls these photo-poems, "phoems", with a few of these becoming greeting cards. Not all of the poems and stories are paired with an image or photo. As my journey to complete this book of images progressed, other experiences began to take shape, so as to fill in missing portions of the book's narrative, I added a few more poems into this book.

The further I moved along the spiritual path, I began to notice how things fell into place way too frequently to be called coincidences. I began to question the how and why of things, especially what is called love. Where did it come from and more importantly, why do some people manifest it differently from others, which inevitably led me to revisit what is called God. I found that God is individually personal and that I and others must seek our own answers on our own spiritual path. I am finding that my perception of what God is, is also changing as Holy Spirit, the Essence Of God, leads me deeper and deeper within my true self, Soul, searching for Truth.

I have found that Holy Spirit continually manifests Itself, not only in this physical world, but also throughout all the higher worlds of God's creation. It is through being consciously aware, that I am beginning to perceive Holy Spirit sustaining all life and working through each one of us. It takes a real effort, to see through the problems of this life, all to open one's eyes to the inner workings of Divine Spirit.

This book is based on a few years of my experiences and within these pages, I will share how Divine Spirit has led me on my sacred journey in the seeking of God, so that it may somehow encourage other seekers on their own sacred journey. My thoughts within this book do not speak for any spiritual practice, path, teacher, guide, religion nor are they intended to supplant one's own understanding of God.

Some of the guidance Divine Spirit has given me is told through poems or stories of experiences from both the outer and inner worlds. It is through listening to the whispers, the tuning in to Holy Spirit, that I have been guided on a spiritual path to God, which is different from the one I was born into. As one gains more trust in Spirit, and Spirit begins to trust you, your heart opens wide, becoming a Divine Channel, allowing Its message to be heard in the lower worlds, GOD LOVES ALL.

To The Light Giver

The Creative Flow Of Divine Spirit

Spirit trickles through the cracks,
filtered by my imperfect mind.
Bringing forth a simple message,
one that can not be confined.

Awakening inner talents,
to me otherwise unknown.
Using words of tale and rhyme,
to tell of my true path home.

As I experience Spirit's voice,
these poems or stories begin.
As a spiritual exercise,
flowing from deeply within.

To where do the messages,
contained within these stories go?
It is only for you the reader,
to quietly reflect and know.

Or daily life may come about,
to pass these on to folks in need.
Something in which to comfort them,
this planting of Divine Spirit's seed.

Dear reader of these poems and stories,
study the messages contained within.
Spirit finding ways to flow through you,
as new experiences now begin.

After The Storm

In a vivid dream experience, I found myself on a small boat in the middle of a wind-swept ocean's night. The boat was being battered by waves from a fierce storm close to the towering, black stone cliffs of a near shore. The lightning and thunder were almost continuous, with the cliffs being almost constantly illuminated by the lightning, with the wind howling across angry, white-capped ocean waves. For some reason, I had no fear, but a deep inner sense of peace, a wonderment, as I witnessed an angry sea battering high rock cliffs during a violent night storm.

The scene then changed to one of a quiet sun-drenched beach with the cliffs meeting a tranquil sea. It seemed to be the very same shore of the night before, only that the storm had broken off some of the rocks from the cliff face, and with the continuous battering of the ocean, smoothing over, polishing the rough edges of the rocks to a lustrous shine on the shore. I found myself following a man of medium height, bearded, dark- skinned middle-aged man dressed in a brown monk's robe, walking along the shore where the ocean's gentle waves lapped at the newly uncovered rocks. I think he was aware of me as I followed him and watched him occasionally picking up a sparkling pebble that had caught his eye and be placed in his robe's pocket.

The dream faded out as I woke for my day in the physical world and recorded the experience. I found it a coincidence, as I was exploring a new and very different spiritual path from that which I was born into, which led to a poem of my interpretation of Holy Spirit's efforts to awaken Soul.

After The Storm

As Soul is battered about,
during a stormy dark night.
The powerful waves of God's love,
can be an awe inspiring sight.

Relentlessly battering away,
at my hardened heart and mind.
It is God's love ever reaching,
for that which is hidden inside.

The ages pass and the spark of God,
its golden light now from cover.
Finds a gentler wave of God's love,
guiding Soul to rediscover.

Soul's journey to its true home,
my spiritual guide is to teach.
For I am no longer walking alone,
along the Light drenched sandy beach.

Soul's Journey Home

There came a point in my life,
being quite sincere.
The question I had asked,
"What am I doing here?"

Usually when my life,
had received a thrown stone.
Or when I was troubled,
and seemingly all alone.

I turned outwardly,
seeking to explain the odd.
It leading me inward,
to find a path to God.

Approaching many crossroads,
uncovering clues as I slowed.
This quest leading me onto,
little used paths to a single road.

Extending across time and space,
I received a very personal sign.
That which became known to me,
as guidance from Spirit Divine.

Impressing on my consciousness,
when mind's grip was at its least.
From Its slumber now awakened,
I, Soul, have been released.

To discover that which is,
inside and all around.
Holy Spirit revealed,
as the Light and the Sound

The Well

Soul feels the fear through the mind's eye,
as the mind knows what Soul must try.

To touch that well of sound and light,
that which is hidden from mind's sight.

The deeper inside one's self Soul goes,
with the Teacher's help, Divine love flows.

Reaching the Source finally at peace,
All fears and doubts are forced to cease.

Soul is given the choice to travel on or stay,
whether it may help other Souls find their way.

For Soul's co-work with God is a sight to behold,
watching other Seekers as they joyously unfold.

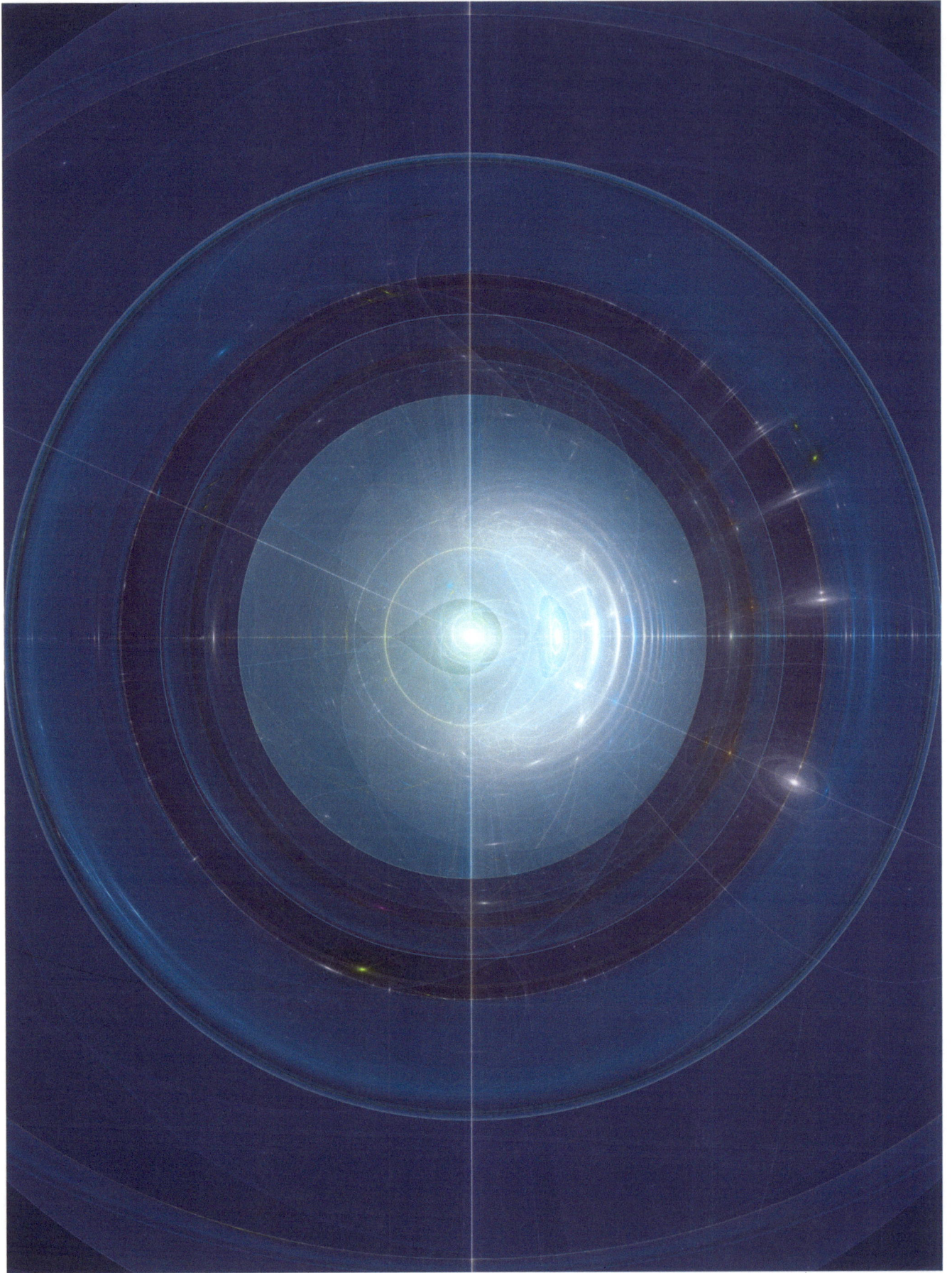

Soul

It seems to me, that where ever I turned to reading various texts, I came across "my Soul", "your Soul" or just "Soul". At some intuitive level, I felt Soul was the real ME, or true self. So just what is Soul? How was it created, by whom and for what purpose? Always questions for my Teacher. Over the course of a week's contemplation, the lessons took form in 2 poems.

In the poem, "Soul", it speaks of a golden mirror. When I was ready, this mirror, one that seems to be composed of Divine Spirit, allowed me to behold my reflection, seeing what others see, the real me as Soul, a unique being of pure Light and Love radiating outward. The only way that I could describe the form that I saw in this mirror, and that this is my perception filtered through my lower mind, is that of a unique star-like snowflake or a fuzzy undefined ball of cotton, with its center burning white hot and transitioning from white hot to bright yellow as It radiates the Love of Holy Spirit outwardly.

The poem, "Young Children Of The Light", tells of a chance encounter with newly created Souls beginning their own journey back to God.

Soul

What is it that which we call Soul,
made up of in parts or as whole?

Not using the earthly senses or the mind,
I am using perception of an inner kind.

Guided by my Teacher to clearly see,
reflected truth as to what Soul must be.

Within a golden mirror shining white,
shows an image of a wondrous sight.

A formless being burning bright,
as a spark of God's divine light.

As I beheld my Self in the looking glass,
memories returned of my distant past.

A new awareness of how I became,
forged from within God's eternal flame.

An existence that knew of no human bounds,
only God's love and the light and the sound.

From an awakening within Spirit's golden glow,
I know myself to be a child of God and as Soul.

Young Children Of The Light

While walking beside my Teacher,
along a temple's waist-high wall.
I heard a sound like that of a roar,
waters rushing over a waterfall.

Throughout the surrounding mists,
of Divine Spirit glowing white.
Appeared many luminous,
finer points of golden Light.

Marveling at the raw beauty,
of these and others of ITs kind.
Newly created sparks of God,
wild and otherwise undefined.

By extending to them,
my formless cupped hand.
One delicate Soul,
did gently land.

A wave of Love flowed from myself,
to this precious little one.
Welcoming It on Its journey,
innocent of worlds yet to come.

As I lifted my hand,
for my Teacher to see.
The Soul began to rise,
drifting away from me.

Drawn close to the Teacher,
this child seemed to delight.
To joyously dance in the flow,
of this great Soul's golden Light.

As the Teacher looked on,
the children seemed to know.
To follow Divine Spirit,
into the worlds below.

Once Soul has its lessons learned,
the Teacher will once again meet.
Guiding each Soul to its true home,
Soul's return journey now complete.

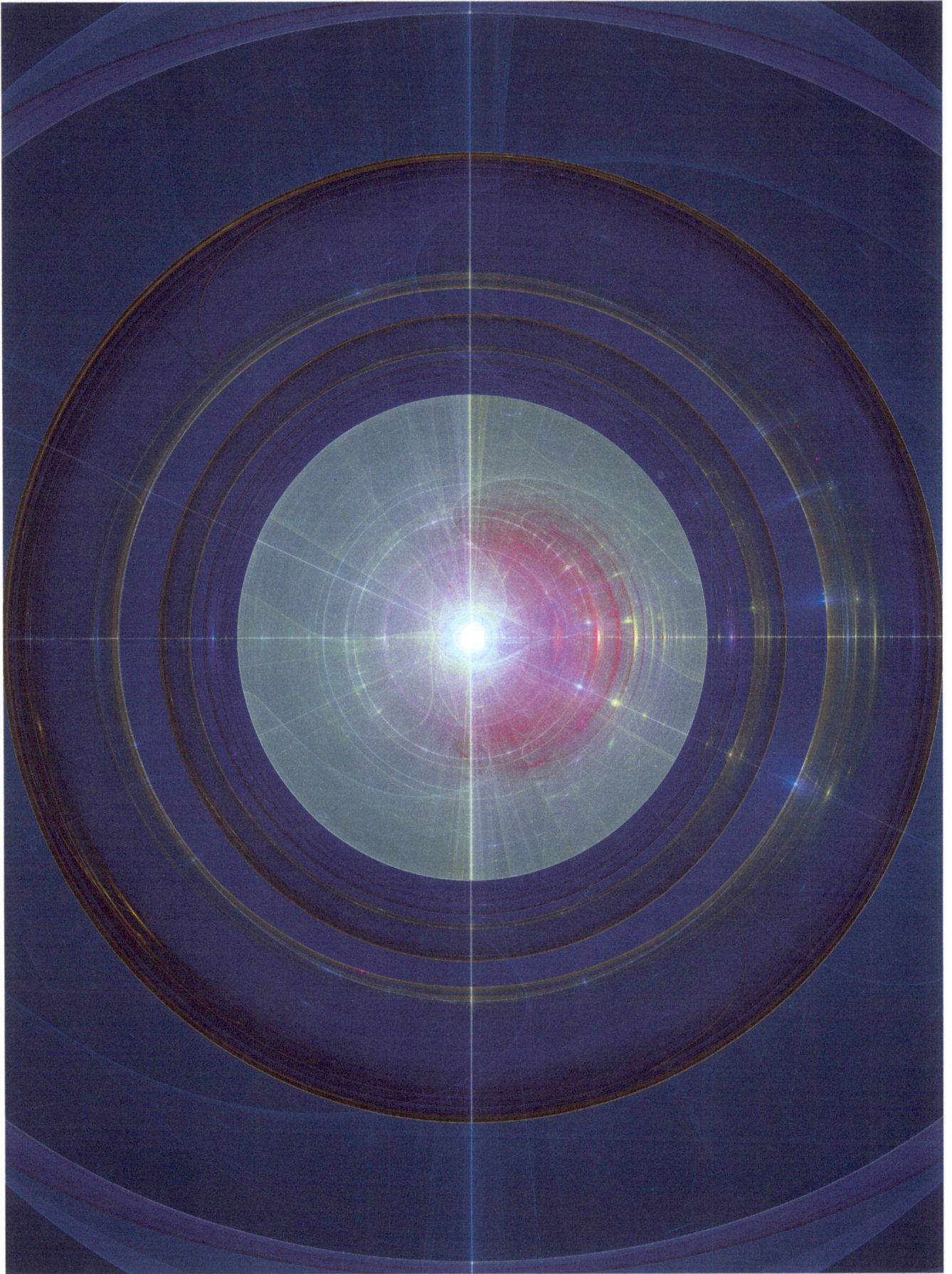

Road Rage

Some highway drivers are,
courteous and aware.
Others are ignorant,
and don't even care.

Some bullying drivers,
use hostility to lend fear.
In a hurry home to those,
whom they hold very dear.

Sometimes I am surprised,
that I made it home alive.
Due to the decisions I made,
while on my return drive.

Detachment and balance,
are hard to remember.
While swerving to avoid,
another one's fender.

But I must remember,
to join cause with effect.
Before starting something,
in which I may later regret.

Now staring back at me,
in the rear view mirror.
My ego blatantly exposed,
Teacher's lessons become clearer.

Echoes

Echoes from forgotten experiences,
tough lessons from my distant past.
Resonate by shaping me now,
giving form to the die as I am cast.

Knowing how far that I have come,
and yet travel further I must go,
Realizing I have barely begun,
on this path that Soul seems to know.

Subtly guided to a qualified Teacher,
preparing my Self for him to arrive.
His showing me the of ways of Spirit,
so that I may become more alive.

With the Teacher's guidance,
 I slowly became more aware.
Of Divine Spirit flowing through me,
perceiving God's love everywhere.

Divine Spirit is ever expanding,
seeking different forms of expression.
It only requires that Soul accept,
Its spiritual growth and mission.

Never pushing me beyond,
what my unique talents can bear.
Instead allowing me to choose,
the manner and method to share.

Its continued spiritual growth,
balances the binding karma of Its past.
Emerging from a mold now broken,
Soul's hard fought freedom is gained at last.

A River

      While on a day trip in the Adirondack country of New York State, the opening sentence of the poem below, began to manifest as I drove down a road that followed alongside the Mohawk River. Drawn by its waters, I found a scenic pull off, and began taking pictures to capture the beauty of the moment by the river. While taking those pictures, I noticed a few ducks floating lazily on the currents of the river, avoiding the shoals and large rocks found within their path. Not unlike Soul, as It tries to find It's way back to God. I had asked my spiritual guide a question, "What happens to Love, once given and received, how does that Love return to God, to be renewed?"

A River

As Divine Spirit radiates outward,
from the awakened to the aimless planes below.
Perceptive Souls uniquely express God's love,
their inner light becoming an intense glow.

An open heart accepting a gift of love,
what happens to this love that was allowed to flow?
Once manifested on this physical plane,
how does It return to God, how does It go?

Looking for examples on this earthly plane,
observing that water collects, small streams form.
Often converging into large rivers,
turbulent waters flowing on a path to transform.

Awakened Souls united with Spirit,
returning to the origin of.
Soul's true home within the stillness,
the Ocean of Mercy and Love.

The Loss Of A Loved One

As this poem gained form, it is for all of the people who are with loved ones going through all the stages of cancer, life threatening conditions or the ones who are at their later stages in life or have passed. This poem may be for the loss of any Soul, whomever has shown you love.

The Loss Of A Loved One

Very few words can bring comfort,
to those feeling sorrow and pain.
Of loosing a loved one who is,
no longer of this earthly plane.

Their demise leaves an emptiness,
deep within your troubled heart.
Caused by those shared experiences,
and by the feelings they impart.

As this unique Soul departs,
this earthly plane for those above.
Their gift we will miss the most,
was their way of giving love.

Take comfort in knowing,
lessons this Soul has learned.
For they are on a path of light,
to a place which they have earned.

So how does one carry on now that they,
and their loved one is physically apart?
Try opening yourself to Divine Spirit,
letting Its Love gently sooth your grieving heart.

Cousin

My cousin had for over a year gone through chemo-therapy for stage 4 lung cancer. The treatments and radiation had caused the cancer to disappear, but after a few months the cancer slowly returned and gained strength. I received a thank you note for a poem that I wrote for her. The poem had arrived during a stressful day, giving her a moment of solace. She remarked, "I now cherish the quiet moments, where I can feel God, wrapping His arms around me with a comforting hug." My cousin passed away about a month after receiving the poem. At her funeral service, where she wrote her own eulogy, she passed on a timeless message for those of us still here on this earth, regardless of one's Spiritual path or practice.

"It is with selfless service to others, that we come to know God on a deeper level". Peggy Minton

She will be missed by all.

Cousin

To a cousin whom I am only now,
beginning to spiritually know.
Watching your faith in God,
as it continues to grow.

Dwelling not on your,
inevitable earthly plight.
Instead finding solace,
in God's heavenly Light.

It is through your Teacher,
you have quietly heard,
The kingdom of God within,
and His eternal Word.

Child of God with your time on earth,
now coming to an end.
May God's Love give you strength,
on your journey to transcend.

Last Goodbye

My Mom had a stroke and was found about thirty-six hours later on her living room floor, still alive. Being a stubborn old farm gal, she hung on and after two weeks of driving the hospital staff absolutely crazy, by literally running up and down several flights of stairs ... at age seventy, she was released back home under her own supervision. The stroke did not affect her motor skills or memory, but did trash her speech center. A CT scan showed a black hole about the size of a golf ball, where speech processing was thought to exist in the center of her brain. I figured my Mom still had some unfinished business on this earth with friends and family, still having something to contribute to our spiritual education, even though some found it hard to communicate with her. Mom cut her suburban lawn with a self-propelled walk behind lawnmower for over seventeen years after the stroke. After bouts of pneumonia and congestive heart failure finally caught up with her, her health declined to the point of being placed in Hospice. It was at that time that I remembered a dream that I had three years before she passed away.

The Last Goodbye

A loved one struggled no more,
knowing that her time drew near.
It was during a night dream,
that my Mom did appear.

During a moonless dark night,
Mom stepped onto a path well worn.
I watching her as she walked by,
leaving this world seemingly torn.

Between whether to stay or go,
hesitating and unsure.
Drawn towards a distant white light,
knowing its invitation is pure.

As this Soul passed I called out,
"Goodbye, I love you Mom"
"Goodbye, I love you too",
she said, now very calm.

Ever drawn into waiting arms,
of recognized loved ones passed.
Continuing on her journey,
free of this earthly plane at last.

Shedding tears not for my loss,
but of her joy at the sight.
As she and others encircled,
within God's Heavenly Light.

God Will Show Each Of Us Our Own Way

        I had been contemplating on the issue of when Soul passes from this earth world into the higher spiritual planes of God; of what is left behind and also what is kept as part of Soul. Those of us still on this earthly plane, have the memories of even the littlest things of what that Soul did, of how they brought to us a subtle awareness of their love and how that love touched those around them.

        I wrote part of an eulogy for my Mom's funeral in which I posed a question, "People remember how we each gave out love, that is why we are here to honor my Mom. So, is it our purpose of why we are here on this earth, to better learn to give out God's love that flows through each of us? Maybe it is to recognize God's guiding hand in this world and help Him make it a better place by allowing His love to shine through each of us."

God Will Show Each Of Us Our Own Way

"Why am I here?",
a pleading question sometimes asked.
During a hard lesson learned,
remembering others of times past.

Do you remember the infant,
looking at you with its first gaze?
Feeling a passed gift of love,
as you looked on in amaze.

Do you remember a loved one,
during their earthly last days?
Their loving heart shining bright,
giving out love in many ways.

What are the lessons learned,
taught to us by that Soul now gone?
By their gift of uniquely giving,
their love now withdrawn.

Could it be that each of us,
from the time of our birth.
Are to be a window for God's love,
to shine through onto this earth?

How does one express divine love,
ITS essence in every breath we take?
God's love is ours to manifest,
using our talents if we are awake.

Love, ever driving one to God,
Soul becoming more aware.
Divine Spirit and our Teacher,
guiding Soul with love and care.

These experiences of God's love,
slowly and gently purify Soul.
Until one becomes a clear window,
through which divine love can purely flow.

The question, "Why am I here?"
was the first proposition asked.
Awakened, "Why I am here!"
is now the spiritual task.

Within those moments of Stillness,
God showing each our own way.
Of how to know God our Self,
each moment of every day.

A Sunset

In the weeks leading up to a Vermont Spiritual Seminar, I had a familiar restlessness, its cause I found difficult to define. On that weekend, I was too wound up to attend most of the Saturday round tables and spiritual discussions and found my self walking around the Burlington waterfront park just outside the Seminar facility. With sunset approaching, I noticed that all along the water's edge people were gathering. An almost hushed excitement seemed to be all around. I brought out my camera and started photographing the sequence of the setting sun over the bay with the Adirondack mountains in the distance. Looking around, there seemed to be an almost palpable sense of peace that had overcome the crowd. Even the dogs people had brought down to the waterfront park were sitting on hind legs, watching the sun set. Catching an-other's eye and with a nod of their head, a perceptive knowing passed between us as though acknowledging the gift of a sunset to subtly awakened the inner Self.

I found my restlessness had dissipated somewhat and could sense and better define the flavor of Divine Spirit flowing throughout the seminar on Sunday. This poem began to form weeks after the Vermont seminar, as reflected on all the seminar participants and the creative environment of the seminar. In a moment of God's creativity, listen inwardly to Its silence.

A Sunset

What is it that stirs within one,
about the making of a sunset?
Inspiring a portion of the mind,
reminding one to not forget.

To hold dear the special moment,
one's Self overcome with peace.
Following the setting sun,
Soul is seeking Its release.

From the daily challenges,
lessons that each of us face.
Some harsh experiences,
very difficult to embrace.

To become aware of one's problems,
that may be presently set aside.
Created beauty touching one,
somewhere deeply inside.

During times of personal problems,
that just never seem to go away.
It is during a sunset's movement,
that Soul follows the Light's ray.

What of the beauty of a setting sun,
an experience shown to us from above?
It is with gratitude that I can recognize,
the subtle healing power of God's love.

Messengers Of The Light And Sound

One of the many speakers at a weekend's spiritual seminar that I attended, told of an ancient story, "The Cracked Vessel." There are many versions of this timeless story, with no one version being the original or its original author known. The lessons are the same now as then.

A fellow seminar attendee had also heard the speaker at the seminar tell of a story of, "The Cracked Vessel." Kathrine explained that she was moved to tears because she too, felt unworthy and that she was not doing enough to spread the message of Divine Spirit. How little did she realize what her selfless efforts of Love have become. This message is for her and others like her.

Messengers Of The Light And Sound

Hidden behind an earthly veil,
are Soul's memories of Its past.
Spirit striving to remind one,
that God's love is beyond vast.

Soul returning to this lower world,
willing to endure another stay,
Soul's has accepted Its mission,
to help God-seekers find their way.

Doubting Holy Spirit's intentions,
with one's talents this time given.
Following the Teacher's guidance,
to serve God, Soul is thus driven.

As one's mind is sometimes too focused,
on the task that makes many demands.
Some may not be conscious of God's love,
as it flows through one and expands.

Contacting those ready to hear of God's love,
sincere hearts calling out to be found.
It is the least of the messengers who sing,
the sweetest song of the Light and of the Sound.

The Earth-Spirit Expo

Occasionally I stop by some "Psychic or Spiritual Fair" and can feel the palpable presence of Divine Spirit as some sort of current or energy flowing around the venue itself and from individual vendors and attendees themselves.

The Earth-Spirit Expo

Folks come from all around,
to this establishment each year.
Guided by some inner nudge,
or by a blurb that they might hear.

Catching a talk about astrology,
or mischievous game playing with the mind.
Or of personal inner and outer health,
energies of the Earth-related kind.

So what do these Souls want,
for what do they truly seek?
Some subtle inner direction,
that is spiritually unique?

Feeling Divine Spirit's influence,
as it winds it's way around us all.
I encountered that here today,
at The Vineyard Banquet Hall.

Spirit Hawk

A spiritual seeker at the "The Earth-Spirit Expo," had inquired how these poems took shape or form. While on my way home from the Spirit Expo I noticed a large red tail hawk floating on the rising wind currents. I contacted my seeker friend and gave him a little homework to complete the poem below, so that it might allow him to become more aware of Divine Spirit in our daily lives.

Spirit Hawk

As the hawk searches for food,
from dawn to early night.
So too does Soul search for,
the Sound and Light.

As an eagle soars higher,
almost from physical sight.
So too does Soul soar,
on wings of spiritual flight.

> You can fill in the rest!
> Have Fun!
> (Hint: BE the Wind)

Is beauty, cause or effect?
(Editor: Go ask Keats), (Author: Go inwardly and ask Holy Spirit)

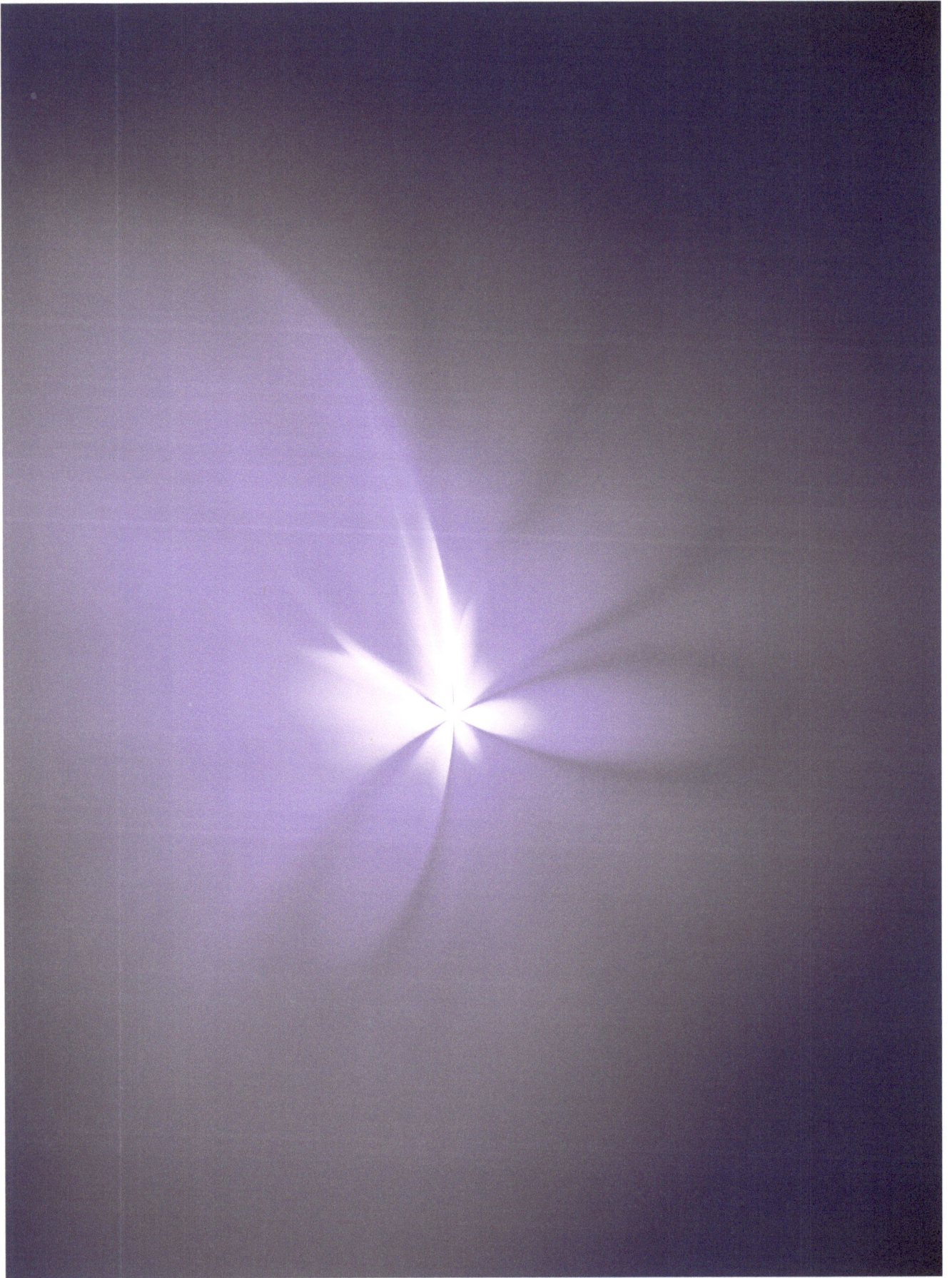

Wild Violet

Music.

What is it about a lyric, instrument, voice or melody that sometimes stirs something within one? It may be while one is attending a spiritual service that one opens oneself inwardly and allow Holy Spirit to awaken Soul. I mostly listen to blues/rock, but sometimes stray to jazz or even Irish classical, depending on what I am working with at the moment. It is as though the singer or group's talents, collectively or individually, bring about a resonance within oneself. It was one night that I was listening to a movie's musical score, that I found the singer's voice gave the song's lyrics a special meaning.

Wild Violet

With her voice and melody,
the inner self leaves behind.
The chaos and distractions,
that plague the outer mind.

Going deeper within one's self,
following her lyric of the song.
This Soul discovered something,
most others knew all along.

Her song of the Divine message,
artfully contained within.
To follow your heart to God,
and may that Journey never end.

The Little Inflight Airplane Mechanic

It seems that spiritual seminars allow one to absorb Divine Love and sometimes, unbeknownst to ourselves, nature's creatures sense this flow of Love.

I had arrived a few hours early to the airport and decided to get something to eat. While I was waiting for my food at the main food court, I notice a lot of small birds seemingly trapped inside the airport main lobby. As I waited to place my order, I mused that maybe the birds were the airline's on-the-wing mechanics to repair airplanes after take off. I ordered a few simple buttered rolls and found my gate at the the other end of the airport. While waiting in the deserted seating area for a plane that was not due to depart for quite a few hours, I munched away on one of the rolls while I read an American western novel.

Engrossed in the book, I almost didn't notice a fluttering of wings on the top of the seat to my left. When I looked over, I thought, "Strange, I thought I heard a bird's wings flapping." I went back to reading my book, when I heard a chirp at my feet. Slow and carefully, I peeked around my book and gazed down at the floor. There, hopping around looking for more of the crumbs that I had inadvertently dropped, was a sparrow. I grinned at the wonder of it. I had the roll in my hand and began to slowly break off a few crumbs and let them fall to the floor. The sparrow, brave little thing that it was, hopped over and began to eat the crumbs. I had my camera and took a picture of it on the floor eating the crumbs.

34

I wonder ....

I began to move slowly, dropping more crumbs to keep the sparrow occupied. I was able to get within inches of this little one, trying to see it I could get it to eat from my hand. The bird looked hesitant, so I left it a few more crumbs and watched it eat its fill. It preened itself, looked at me, let out a chirp, maybe a Thank You in bird-speak, then flew away.

It occurred to me, that some of us are like this little one. We are fed the crumbs of Truth that God drops to one here on this earth and come so very close, but are too skeptical to accept His offered hand.

The Little Inflight Airplane Mechanic

Waiting in the terminal for my plane,
with a generous amount of time to spare.
A sparrow on almost silent wings,
fluttered onto the top of next chair.

I mused that this little one and his friends,
were the airline's best choice to repair.
An airplane should it need the attention,
of a capable mechanic in midair.

As my little friend hopped to the floor,
looking for another forgotten crumb.
I broke apart my half-eaten roll,
between index finger and thumb.

While observing my feathered friend,
bird-walking in search of more to eat.
I reflected that I to erratically searched,
for crumbs of Truth while at God's feet.

Lured closer by the crumbs in hand,
close enough to within finger's touch.
My little friend became hesitant,
of something that offered so much.

Looking up at me with gratitude,
chirping for the generous meal share.
My little in-flight airplane mechanic,
then winged its way into the air.

To Just BE

As a door is allowed to open,
to an expanse intimate yet vast.
Indistinct memories illumined,
connected to Soul's distant past.

Passing into a silent world,
of foggy misty golden light.
My incessant questions,
had become a profane slight.

By the gradual quieting of Soul,
within that stillness I began to hear.
A whispered almost silent sound,
as the Word of God became clear.

Soul slowly becomes part of,
the dynamic worlds of God.
At times Soul's unique expression,
of ITs message may seem very odd.

As God's love seeps deeper into Soul,
to the Divine laws Soul must agree.
In that moment of oneness with Spirit,
Soul now knows how to just BE.

Love IS

Love IS: Charity, compassion and kindness, all humanly discerned,
Outer reflections of inner lessons learned.

Love IS: The unique wave of light emanating from Soul,
An unshakable trust felt through Its intense golden glow.

Love IS: The inner resonance deep within the stillness of Soul,
The Silence giving strength to the sound and light's ebb and flow.

Love IS: That we exist to express God's call,
Being aware that Divine Love sustains all.

A Gathering Of Friends

Spiritual seminars, when I can attend them, have a theme or an energy that winds its way through the day or whole weekend. To me, this is Holy Spirit showing each Soul some aspect of Itself. It is my nature to sit back in some dark corner and observe the play of Spirit. While watching from the top of an auditorium bleacher, it was this experience of watching Souls say goodbye to each other, that this poem came to mind.

A Gathering Of Friends

Friends from all around this wide world,
gather in the Fall of each year.
Attending workshops and round-tables,
from spiritually like-minded they hear.

Discussions of practical techniques,
to enliven one's search for Truth.
Or take to heart the stories of Travelers,
veterans of spiritual sleuth.

Explorers seeking reality,
from within inner worlds of old.
Teachers at the Temples of Light and Sound,
guiding Souls to spiritually unfold.

Watching unnoticed from a place above,
as friends departed the seminar below.
I could sense a renewed purpose in the,
lingering farewells as each were aglow.

As this gathering of worldwide friends,
draws to a conclusion for this year,
Many of us and our new found friends,
go our separate ways with a tear.

Be not sad as we make our journey home,
distanced from each other by physical sight.
For each will greet the other on the inner planes,
recognized by their unique heavenly Light.

Young Love's Eternal Song

While attending a spiritual seminar, there was a talk given by a young couple, titled, "Awakening The Golden Heart." I found it easier to tune in to them, by closing my eyes and listening to the subtle nuances of their voices, as they spoke from their hearts. As they expressed themselves, sharing how they find bits of love in everyday things, I could feel a palpable wave of love flow from them to the audience. By the knowing expressions of others in the audience, they felt the couple's expression of love and responded by opening their own hearts, recognizing the flow of love and returning it to the young speakers. I could perceive another, yet finer wave of love that began to make Its presence known. Divine Spirit being drawn to the many Souls' pure and open hearts, began to fill the room with waves of God's Love. It seemed to me that these waves of love were like subtle air currents, each Soul became a unique channel for Divine Love to be expressed into this world.

As a side note, at some of the spiritual seminars, I found some of the speakers were from foreign countries and their English is highly accented. I tried this same tuning in technique, letting go of my mind's inability to comprehend some of the words and I experienced each Soul's unique way of expressing Divine Love.

Young Love's Eternal Song

A young couple put into words,
the awakening of the golden heart.
Sharing personal experiences,
of how everyday things play their part.

In recognizing God's Divine plan,
creative lessons to lead home each Soul.
It is this awareness that opens one's heart,
Divine Spirit allowing each to play a role.

As I and others perceived their message of love,
valuing their insight and replying in kind.
Each began to open their own hearts to form,
a wave of love of their own and to find.

Divine Spirit making Itself known,
apparent to hearts open and pure.
Each a channel for Holy Spirit,
God's love flowing uniquely and sure.

Holy Spirit trusting this young couple,
each of their golden hearts beating strong.
As an example of God's creative lessons,
flowing though young love's eternal song.

A Temple of Light

A little known temple of light,
exists in an unthinkable place.
Hidden within an inner plane,
inaccessible by time or space.

At this stage of journey's end,
surrounded by high mountain peaks.
Soul moves along the path to,
Divine Spirit as It seeks.

A gold bound oak entrance door,
only opened by singing HU.
Soul passing through a cleansing shower,
composed of an intense light of white-blue.

Moving through a corridor built,
of large stone blocks of clear glass.
Divine Spirit flowing near,
permitting Soul to pass.

Nearing the temple's parapet,
high above a light-drenched beach.
Soul looks out over a calm ocean,
to a beauty just beyond Its reach.

Sensing a force within Spirit,
the presence of a great Soul nearby.
The Teacher appears shining pure,
an agent of God in these worlds on high.

At last reaching the spiritual planes,
the Teacher welcomes Soul as an old friend.
Soul allowed to experience Divine Spirit,
the essence of God's Love with no end.

Both Souls taking in the beauty,
out over the temple's parapet wall.
Gazing towards an ocean of Light and Sound,
as Divine Spirit flows to all.

Autumn's Mists

      This poem began as a photo while driving to a spiritual seminar in Connecticut. The theme for the seminar had to do with spiritual cycles and how Soul interacts with Holy Spirit within the major and minor cycles. I had been driving along NY Rt 86/17 in the Catskills enjoying how the nearly leafless trees were playing hide-n-peek in the early morning valley fog. One especially long and deep valley presented an excellent opportunity for a photo. A few miles down the road along a river valley, a bald eagle was searching for a riverside meal from a tree top.

Autumn's Mists

Autumn's damp mists herald,
a cycle almost complete.
A call to finish tasks begun,
before Winter's cold sleep.

As Autumn's fallen colored leaves,
are hidden beneath Winter's snow.
A natural time to prepare,
for the next cycle of ebb and flow.

As I mark the completion of,
the spiritual cycle at hand.
Soul looks to a new beginning,
to gradually cross the land.

After reviewing this past year's,
recorded thoughts, goals and deeds.
The obligation re-examined,
guided by Spirit to wherever it leads.

It is the onward journey to God,
that the subtle tests begin anew.
Soul enlivening Its inner strength,
gained by the singing the sacred HU.

The Turning Of A Page

I had signed up months before to attend an early Spring seminar in Rhode Island. As I packed my suitcase the evening before the morning's planned drive, I had not been paying attention to the weather reports, until I stepped outside my door and found 3 inches of wet snow, rapidly accumulating on my truck's windshield. I had heard we were supposed to get a few inches from a nor'easter, but listening to the updated weather report, they said the snow would be over two feet for that coming night. Looking further into the report, the way I had to go through the Catskills, it was forecast to have over three feet by morning.

If I waited to leave until morning, I would be snowed in, missing the seminar. So I loaded my truck with my stuff and left the house at six P.M. The roads were terrible; no plows out, with six inches of rutted hard-packed snow for the first sixty miles, then sleet and rain for the next four hours. Throughout the white knuckle drive, I kept getting the nudge to keep going. It was midnight before I got to the hotel on the other side of the Catskills.

The Turning Of A Page

Driving through a late Winter storm,
my cold steering wheel held in a tight grip.
HU and my Teacher as Co-Pilot,
seat belts tightened aiming for a safe trip.

My distinctive sea-side goal,
it's location hours distant but clear.
The Ocean State spiritual seminar,
held in early March of every year.

Seekers arrived all safe and sound,
introduced to friends both new and old.
Drawn together this weekend,
despite the wind, the rain and the cold.

Looking forward to musicians' songs,
and the message that they impart.
And, of paint brush artists' expressions,
each brought to life by a loving heart.

In a room with the outer works of the Masters,
a Seeker looking for a inner message new.
Eager Souls being guided to God,
uplifted by the singing of HU.

One speaker talked of being a lover of life,
a particularly challenging day-to-day goal.
Another spoke of being a better listener,
to help impart the message of God's Love for Soul.

Still others spoke of simple techniques and insights,
to help one on this Path to spiritually grow.
Giving one tools to better understand,
life's every day problems, or to better show.

How to go deeply within one's heart,
when there are times of unbearable pain.
Or of being aware of your Teacher,
guiding Soul to understand service as a spiritual gain.

Pondering the quietude on the long drive home,
the nor'easter but a memory of Winter's rage.
Seminar insights noted in my Journal Of Life,
now turned to another indifferent empty page.

Travelers On The Road Home

Within the nameless spiritual world,
where God forges from ITS whole.
Emerges a consciousness,
a newly created Soul.

Untested, undeserving,
sent to a spiritual desert.
Picking up sheathed bodies,
to protect Soul from hurt.

Tempering an undisciplined Soul,
with lessons of darkness and light.
Soul's experiences slowly,
begin to open Soul's sight.

The difficult journey back,
to our true home begins.
As Holy Spirit nudges,
us to go deeply within.

Here within these lower planes,
where opposites coexist.
Outward attention is withdrawn,
inwardly to where light does persist.

Guided by the Teacher,
to the Light and the Word.
Soul is drawn to the inner,
by what It has seen and heard.

Deeper into the planes,
where no shadows are cast.
Sometimes seeing others,
Souls from lessons past.

At times coming together,
as a gathering of close friends.
Journeying on different paths,
but once more meeting at the end.

As Soul treads the higher path,
seemingly traveling all alone.
Soul becomes aware of God's love,
as Its companion on the road home.

God Loves All

Over the last few years, I have attended more than a few memorial and funeral services for close relatives and friends of various spiritual paths. The common thread, what people spoke of the most, was how that departed Soul manifested love. Each of those Souls' expressions of love was unique, individualized, like fingerprints. It was the telling of the memories of parent to child, grandchild to grandparent and of a kindness to a stranger, that started a curiosity within my self. I knew that Divine Love was behind this manifested love, regardless of spiritual path, but how was that flow of love so different between not only those that passed, but also with each of us still here in the lower worlds?

I had begun a contemplation on that question one night, and as I began to sing HU, an ancient name for God, I found myself in a corridor that seemed to have a flow of golden white fire all around it. As I peered through what seemed to be huge blocks made of a clear glass, I began to perceive the fire, as the flow of Divine Spirit. On one part of the wall of glass blocks that were polished exceedingly smooth, was what seemed to be a golden mirror. I moved towards it and found that the reflection I was staring at had no arms, legs, head or human body, only a undulating ribbon-like globe of golden light with what looked to be a bright white center, the beauty of Soul's inner light, a spark of God. I began to look more closely at the bright light and found myself falling into that reflection, moving deeper within myself. I reached a point of stillness within Soul, finding the light gently flowing through me. I became aware of a deepening Silence and was drawn towards an ever more beautiful flow of Light, then, not becoming part of, but being absorbed into the Light. I could not tell where Soul ended and Holy Spirit began, I was one with Spirit.

I must pause here to put into words what I perceived as being one with Divine Spirit. In this physical world we are part of an environment. In that environment, the air that we all share by breathing in and out containing atoms of oxygen, nitrogen, carbon dioxide, hydrogen, etc. Imagine if you will, becoming one with that environment, by crossing a boundary of consciousness that allows you to know each atom and the space between them. Taking the next step, come to know all atoms in the physical world, then each particle of light emitted by the sun, then space and time. The mind staggers trying to cope with intimately knowing all things below the spiritual planes, Soul does not. Soul is made from the same stuff as Divine Spirit, but with different purpose. I perceived Divine Spirit as the Life Force to posses a limitless intelligence, unlike Soul which has free will. When Soul is aware of and then allows Divine Spirit to guide us, Soul's purpose becomes the same as Divine Spirit. Again, these are my perceptions.

I sensed that I was flowing downward into the lower worlds, but not alone within this wave of Light. There were other Souls caught up within Its purpose and it was then I recognized the presence of the Teacher. When this wave reached the lower worlds, different streams and infinitely finer threads of light began splitting from within the wave of Light. I began to hear a roaring sound, like that of the thundering of water flowing over an immense waterfall. The streams flowed around and through all life, sustaining and nourishing all things. The finer threads of light, almost as points of light, seemed to find and flow around all Souls. I sensed each Soul using this flow of love differently, by the uniqueness of each personality, inner talent and spiritual maturity. I sensed the beauty of Soul manifesting God's love into the lower worlds and how each Soul is connected to Divine Love.

Awesome!

I sensed, yet another purpose to those almost invisible points of golden light. I found that some Souls, whose inner light shone more brightly than others and seemed to be awakened by the Light, becoming more consciously aware and begin to seek Its Source. Those points of light were showing Soul Its path and Soul being guided by listening to Its loving sound. I found myself back within that corridor of golden light, watching the wave of Divine Spirit continue upwards, returning to the higher spiritual worlds. I began to realize that each Soul is connected to Divine Spirit by Soul's uniquely individual way of expressing love. It is those threads of light, that inner connection to Divine Love and the guidance of the Teacher that allows Soul to begin Its journey back to God. As Soul becomes more consciously aware of that Divine Love as it flows through each of us, it is with our own unique gifts, both inner and outer, that Soul manifests ITs message, Soul exists because of God's love for all.

I Remember

I remember!
Existing in some spiritually plane on high.
Watching!
The waves of Holy Spirit flow gently by.

Perceiving an element within,
the unbreakable golden strands of love.
Woven into the essence of Spirit,
all flowing from God above.

Drawn closer to these golden strands,
Soul is held in Its closest embrace.
Guiding Soul by lessons of light and sound,
helping in Its return to Its birthplace.

Soul entrusting Itself to Spirit,
silent counsel as to the unique goal.
All the while a natural stillness,
begins to exist deep within Soul.

The awareness of Soul's reality,
of being forged from God's Eternal Flame.
Soul's remembrances enlivened,
now knowing from that which It became.

With the Teacher as my companion,
a guiding light of the Way within.
Revealing the high road to God,
the next cycle of my quest to begin.

Like An Ice Cube

At the beginnings of Soul's conscious existence,
too wild to provide God with any assistance.

Carried ever downward leaving God's pure love behind,
Soul's journey of divine discipline is only to remind.

Soul of it's consciousness gracelessly defined,
slowly descending into the lower worlds as designed.

It's downward journey slowly changing It's state,
cast into lower forms so that it can relate.

To the physical guise and thought now intertwined,
Soul is thoroughly and inescapably confined.

To the austerity of the earth world It is bound,
harsh spiritual lessons going 'round and 'round.

It's consciousness lies in a hard frozen state,
cause and effect presently controlling Its fate.

Until Holy Spirit's Light penetrates the imposed dark,
the Teacher's guidance shines God's love onto Soul's spark.

The Holy Fire thawing the coldness that does surround,
Soul being purified by the golden Light and Sound.

While slowly retracing Its steps into worlds above,
Soul is increasingly attuned to God's pure love.

Soul's welcomed return to the higher spiritual planes,
earned by service to God, ridding It of the lower world's chains.

Soul's accepted task of aiding Seekers along the road they trod,
assisting the Teacher in the Seeker's return to God.

The I of Soul

There is a perception of passing through,
of what seemed to be many a thin veneer.
Drawn ever more deeply into,
an infinitely formless white sphere.

Light and vibrations concentrate,
deep within the misty veils,
Sympathetically shielding
Soul's innermost details.

At the very core of Soul lies
the creation of God, a Divine spark.
An essence so absolutely pure,
as to have no defining mark.

Perceiving ITS pure unchanging Light,
and of formless currents within,
into that intimate Stillness,
I am irresistibly drawn in.

Experiencing the unknown and yet,
familiar qualities of this Light,
I realize how Divine Spirit is drawn,
to those same qualities blazing bright.

Flowing through this pure Light of Soul,
Divine Love began to expand.

Then, on some higher level,
something I had yet to understand,
A conscious realization occurs…
the existence of a Divine birthright…

I AM that Stillness,
I AM that spark of Light.

I AM SOUL.

Within The Silence

Soul resonating within the flow,
of Divine Spirit all around.
Experiencing the outer currents,
of the inner core of Light and Sound.

Drawn deeper into the subtle regions,
of Divine Spirit pure and bright.
No longer confined to the shadows
of God's reassuring golden light.

The awakening moment of freedom,
the comprehension of to just BE.
Within the Silence of the Sound,
Soul now consciously does see.

Itself no longer separated from,
or Its existence as a part of.
More precisely, Soul finds Itself,
united as one within Divine Love.

Distinct streams within the light,
flowing from a dynamic source.
Perceived qualities of the boundless,
an all sustaining Life Force.

In this moment, Soul knows freedom,
through Divine Spirit's guidance.
In addition to God's love binding all,
within the Silence.

Within The Silence, All Are One
Within The Silence, ALL IS ONE
Within The Silence, ALL IS TRUTH
Within The Silence, ALL IS LOVE
Within The Silence, FREEDOM GAINED

to be continued,

God, how may I now, truly serve you?

Author's note: The "to be continued" thing has to do with how we never stop spiritually unfolding, always taking the next step, eternally adding to the verses of existing poems or creating new poems from of our own individually unique lessons experienced on our path back to God.

BE One with the Silence

Bibliography

Acknowledgments

  To the Reader; I would like to thank you for taking the time to read the assembled stories and these poems that came about. As I do not respond to requests, I encourage you to go deeper into the heart of God to answer your questions in your search for Truth. Maybe you can write your own stories or poems. May there be a path.

  To the Editor; Joyce, at the start of this endeavor I had only a rudimentary understanding of the English language and none of poetry. Although nowhere near the profound deepness of Keats, or the style of Shakespeare for that matter, you have helped me shape this collection of words into something unique as Soul. Thank you for your guidance.

To The Editor, Joyce Snyder

Thank You: For being the editor of this book,
    correcting the punctuation and words that I mistook.

Thank You: For identifying the chaff and giving it the hook,
    going through red pens while giving a deeper look.

Thank You: For trying to follow some of my gobbledygook,
    editing undeterred regardless of how long it took.

Thank You: For my feeble attempts to not become like Keats,
    helping to clarify a message within these written sheets.

Thank You: Joyce Snyder, Soul to Soul,
    for allowing me to reach Divine Spirit's original goal.

  This book is of my own simple, yet continuously evolving, perceptions of God and is not intended to speak for any spiritual practice, path, teacher, guide, religion or supplant one's own understanding of God. However, I am constantly amazed, humbled and grateful for the lessons gained from both the outer and inner guidance while studying the spiritual path of Eckankar. If you would like to know more about Eckankar, The Path Of Spiritual Freedom, please call 1-800-LOVE-GOD or visit www.Eckankar.org.

www.ingramcontent.com/pod-product-compliance
Lightning Source LLC
Chambersburg PA
CBHW060933150426
42812CB00060B/2649